Eamonn O'Farrell

Contents

What Is Soccer?

Soccer is a kind of sport.
Lots of people like playing soccer.

The Field

Soccer games are played on a grass field. The shape of the field is a rectangle.

But you can play soccer anywhere.

The Team

There are 11 players in a soccer team. They all have jobs to do.

Forwards

Two players try to score goals.

Midfielders

Four players **defend** and **attack**.

Defenders

Four players try to stop the other team from getting a goal.

Goalkeeper

One player tries to stop the other team's ball from going into the net.

Moving the Ball

There are lots of ways to move the ball in soccer.

1. You can kick the ball along the ground.
2. You can kick the ball in the air.

3 You can use your head to hit the ball. This is called **heading**.

4 You can use your hands to throw the ball from the **sidelines**.

How to Kick a Ball

1. Place one foot next to the ball.
2. Swing your other foot back, then swing it forward.
3. Kick the ball with the inside of your foot.

How to Head a Ball

1. Bend your knees.
2. Keep your eyes open.
3. Hit the ball with the front of your head.

Scoring Goals

In a soccer game, you try to get goals. A goal is when the ball goes into the net. The team that gets the most goals is the winner.

You can score a goal with a kick or with a header.

kick

header

You cannot use your hands to get a goal.

Playing Soccer

Look at all the ways you can play soccer!

ANGELLOTTI
10
8
MONTA
SVBN

Glossary

attack to do something so that you beat someone

defend to keep safe from attack

heading bumping the soccer ball with your head

sidelines the edges of the soccer field